W9-AUJ-033

My Eyes

Brian Enslow

Bailey Books
an imprint of
Enslow Publishers, Inc.
40 Industrial Road
Box 398
Berkeley Heights, NJ 07922
USA
http://www.enslow.com

Bailey Books, an imprint of Enslow Publishers, Inc.

Copyright © 2011 by Enslow Publishers, Inc.

Library of Congress Cataloging-in-Publication Data

Enslow, Brian.
  My eyes / Brian Enslow.
      p. cm. — (All about my body)
   Summary: "Simple text and photographs present a story about eyes"—Provided by
publisher.
   Includes bibliographical references and index.
   ISBN 978-0-7660-3813-4 (alk. paper)
   1. Eye—Juvenile literature. 2. Vision—Juvenile literature. I. Title.
   QP475.7.E57 2011
   612.8'4—dc22
                                      2010014875
Paperback ISBN: 978-1-59845-169-6

Printed in the United States of America

052010 Lake Book Manufacturing, Inc., Melrose Park, IL

10 9 8 7 6 5 4 3 2 1

To Our Readers: We have done our best to make sure all Internet Addresses in this book
were active and appropriate when we went to press. However, the author and the publisher
have no control over and assume no liability for the material available on those Internet sites
or on other Web sites they may link to. Any comments or suggestions can be sent by e-mail
to comments@enslow.com or to the address on the back cover.

❂ Enslow Publishers, Inc., is committed to printing our books on recycled paper. The paper
in every book contains 10% to 30% post-consumer waste (PCW). The cover board on the
outside of each book contains 100% PCW. Our goal is to do our part to help young people
and the environment too!

Photo Credits: Shutterstock.com.

Cover Illustration: Shutterstock.com

Note to Parents and Teachers

Help pre-readers get a jumpstart on reading. These lively stories introduce simple concepts
with repetition of words and short simple sentences. Photos and illustrations fill the pages
with color and effectively enhance the text. Free Educator Guides are available for this series
at www.enslow.com. Search for the *All About My Body* series name.

Contents

Words to Know

eagle   eye   fish

Big eyes.
Are these your eyes?

Red eyes.
Are these your eyes?

Fish eyes.
Are these your eyes?

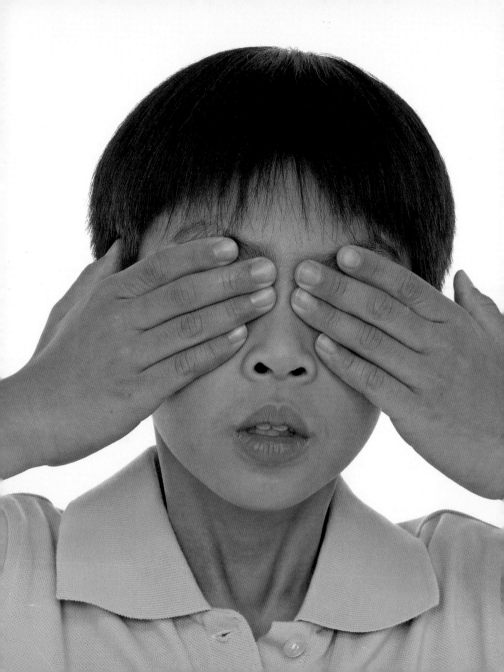

No eyes?

Black eyes.
Are these your eyes?

Eagle eyes.
Are these your eyes?

Dog eyes.
Are these your eyes?

Cat eyes.
Are these your eyes?

New eyes.
Are these your eyes?

Your eyes?

My eyes.

Read More

DeGezzelle, Terri. *Taking Care of My Eyes.* Mankato, Minn.: Capstone Press, 2006.

Klingel, Cynthia Fitterer. *Eyes/Los Ojos.* Strongsville, OH: Gareth Stevens Publishing, 2010.

Web Sites

Enchanted Learning
<http://www.enchantedlearning.com/dictionarysubjects/body.shtml>

Sid Says on PBS Kids
<http://pbskids.org/sid/#/sidSays>

Index

Guided Reading Level: **B**
Guided Reading Leveling System is based on the guidelines recommended by Fountas and Pinnell.

Word Count: **54**